YOU CAN DRAW MONSTERS!

BY DOKTOR MIKAELAUS VON HOFFMAN

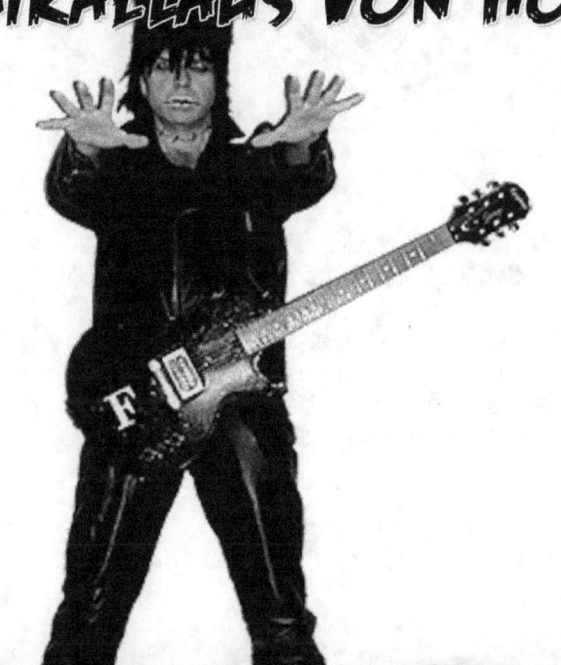

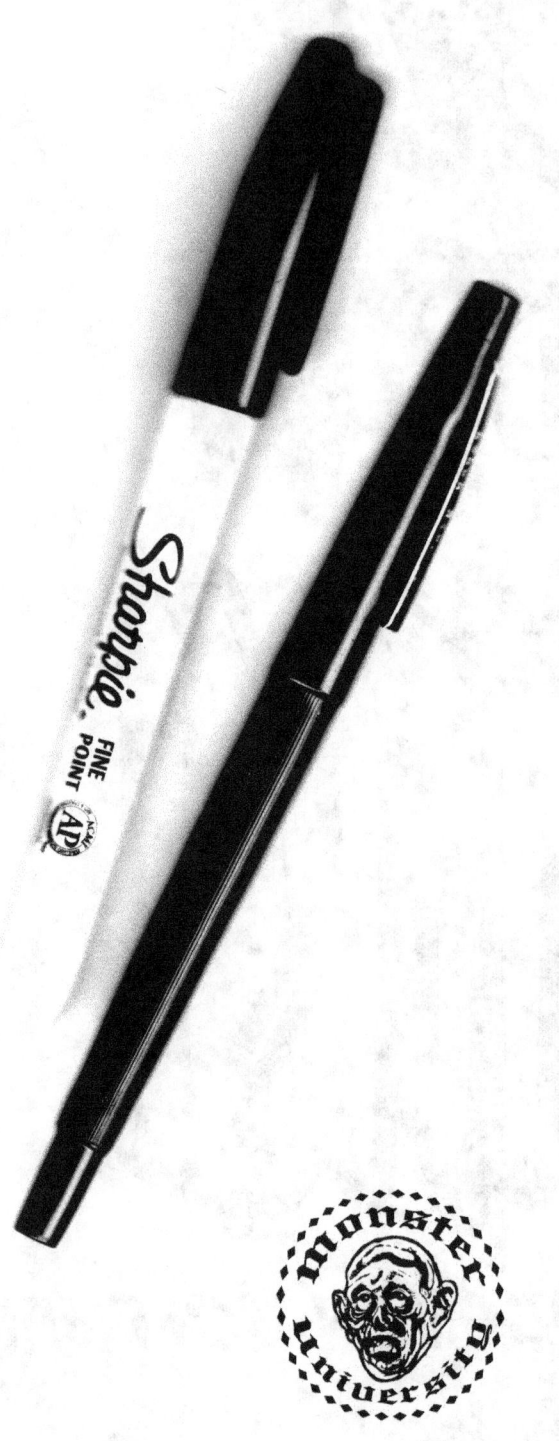

ALL TH' DRAWIN'S IN THIS HERE BOOK WERE DONE WIT TH' CHEAPEST MATERIALS POSSIBLE!

WE USED MARKERS LIKE DOZE ON YER LEFT!

A BIG **SHARPIE** FER BLACKS AN' THICK LINES...

...PLUS A **PAPERMATE** MARKER FER THINNER LINES LIKE HAIR, TEETH, WRINKLES AN' PIMPLES!

ALSO, WE REKKUMEND USIN' EIGHT AND A HALF BY ELEVEN PAPER, GET TH' HEAVY **CARDSTOCK** STUFF!

YEW ARE GONNA HAVE SOME FUN DRAWIN' ICKY MONSTERS ALONG WID OL' VON HOFFMAN, SO LET'S GIT CRACKIN'!

BWA-HA-HA!

ISBN-13: 978-1974364183
ISBN-10: 1974364186

THE #1 SECRET TA DRAWIN' MONSTERS IS THAT YA CAN'T MAKE A MISTAKE! THAT'S WHY THEY'RE MONSTERS! FIRST YA START WID A FUNNY SAUSAGE-SHAPE DAT WE CALL TH' BLOB...

NEXT STEP, DOCTOR FRANKENSTEIN? NOW, BREAK THE OUTLINE WID TH' MOUTH, OR JAW! MAKE IT POKE OUT ON TOP OR BOTTOM! THEN ADD YER PEEPERS, AN' MAKE 'EM DIFFRUNT SIZED, TOO...

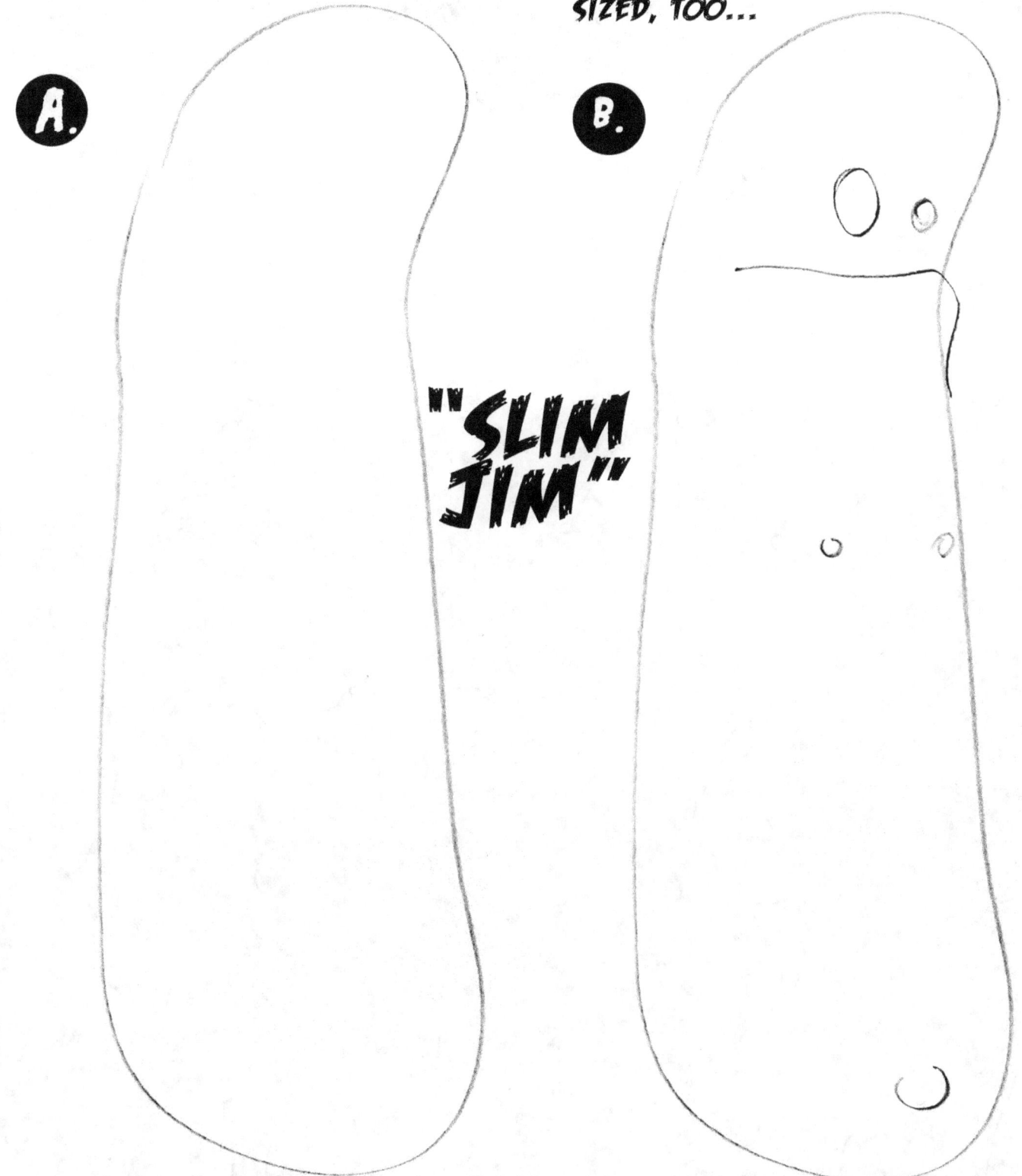

A.

B.

"SLIM JIM"

DIS IS RILLY TH' HARDEST PART! MAKE YER SHAPE STOOPID AN' FUNNY!

DON'T FERGET T' ADD TH' SEXY BITS, FER TH' LADIES IN TH' AUDIENCE!

NOW YA ADD "TUBING" THAT WILL BECOME THE PUNY ARMS AN' DINKY LEGS! DON'T WORRY ABOUT PLACE-MENT, PUT EVERYTHING IN TH' WRONG PLACE! BWAH-HA-HA!

C.

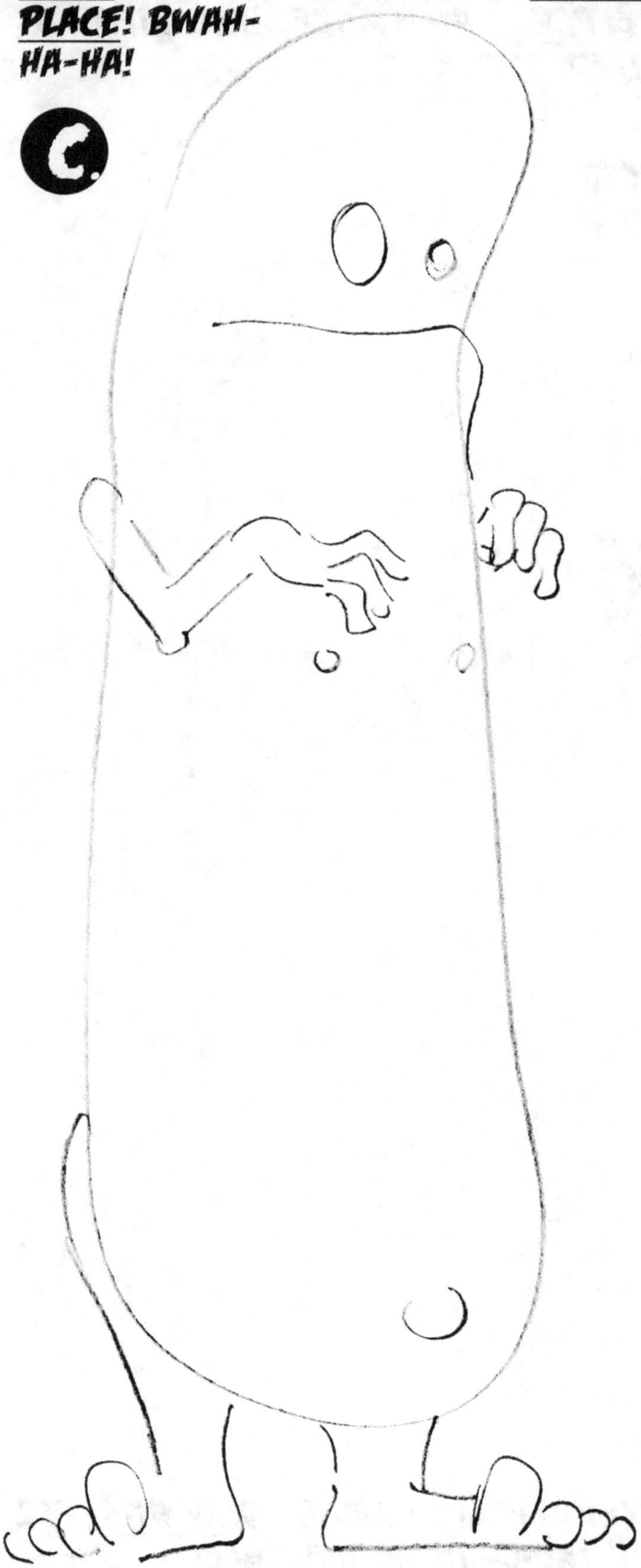

THEN YA START ADDIN' YER MONSTER DETAILINS', LAHK HAIR, BANDAGES, BOLTS, SCARS, LEAKY LIQUIDS, STUBBLE, PIMPLES AN' SO ON! PUT STUFF EVERWHAR!

D.

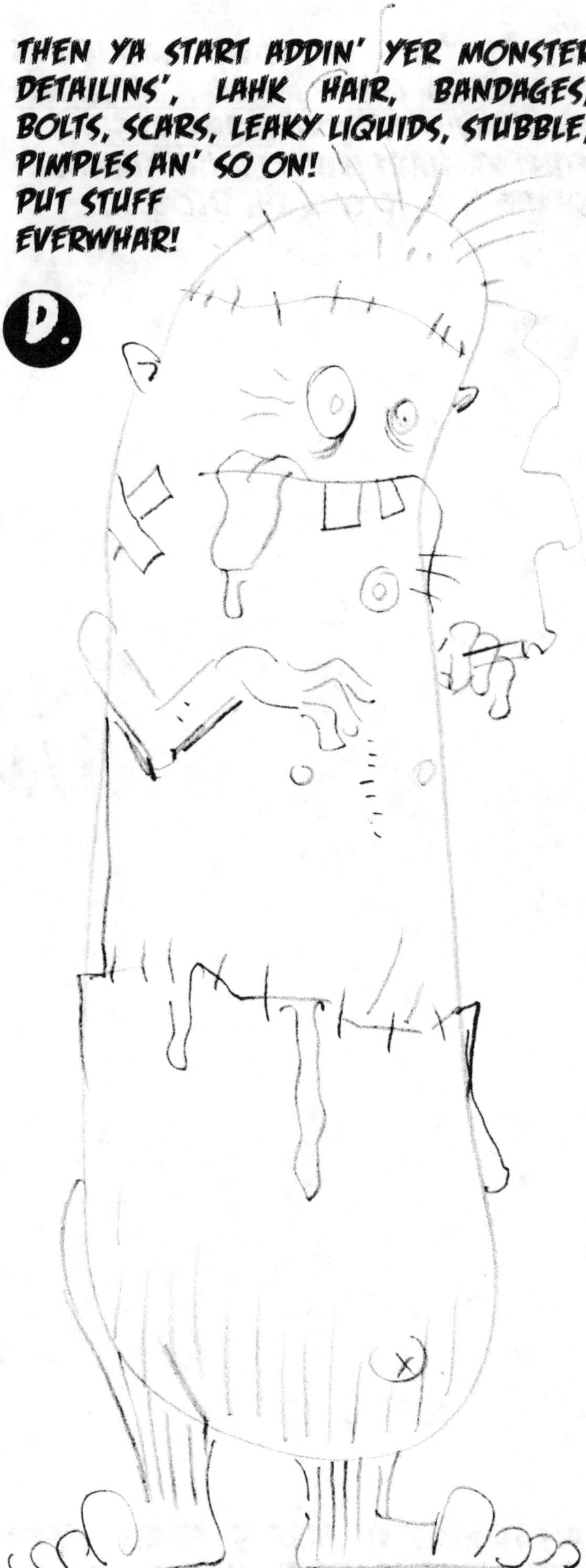

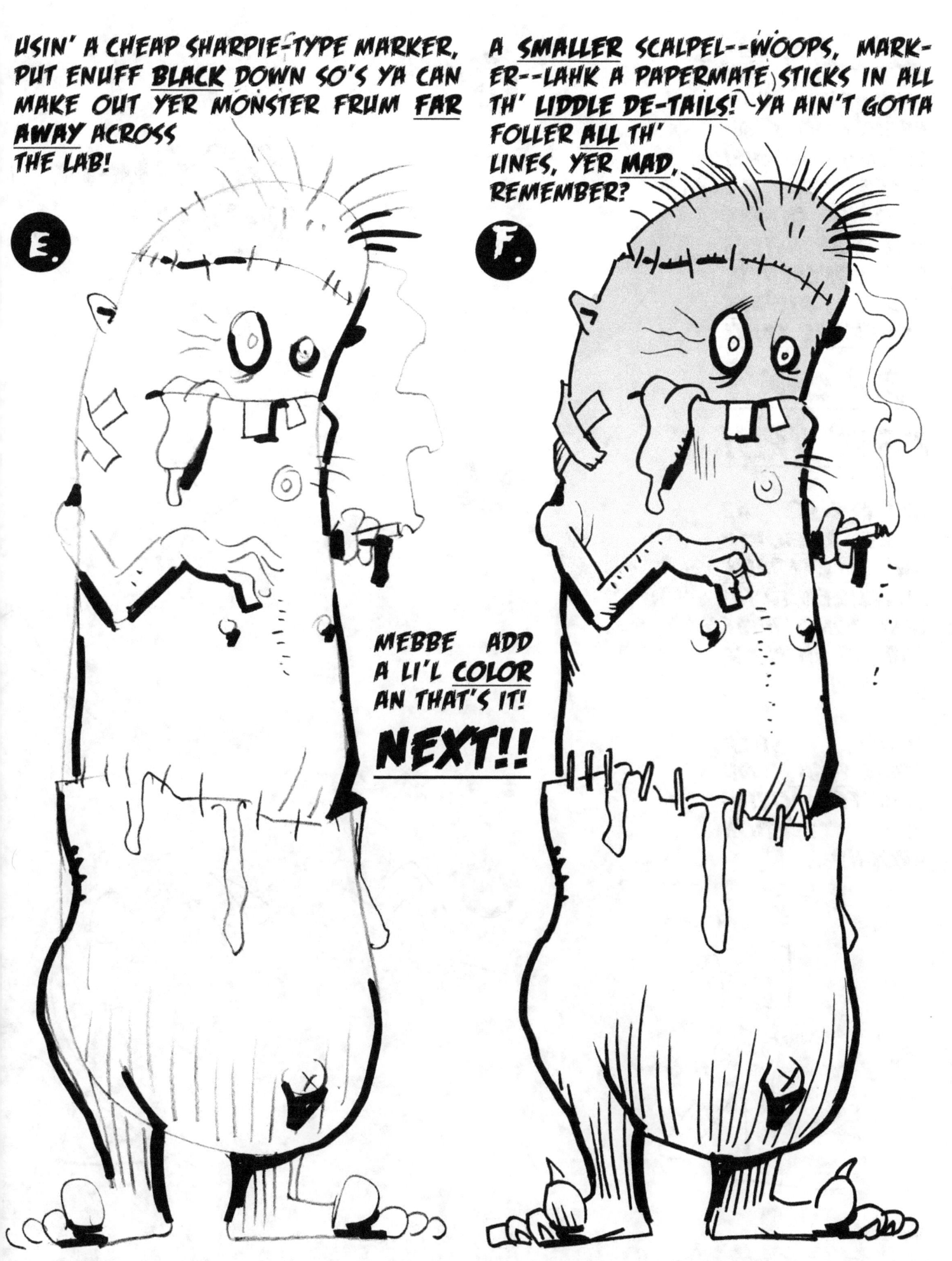

AN' FER YER NEXT MONSTER, TRY ANOTHER DIF-FRUNT GOOFY AN' STOOPID SHAPE! THERE ARE <u>NO</u> WRONG SHAPES WHERE MONSTERS ARE CONCERNED, PALSY! <u>ALWAYS</u> REMEMBER THAT!

YEW CAN'T MESS UP!!!

AN' FER STEP #2 MAKE A <u>MOUTH</u> AN' <u>EYEBALLS</u> JUS' LIKE WID TH' LAST MONSTER! BE SURE TA GIT IT <u>ALL</u> WRONG!

LASTLY, STICK SOME <u>TUBIN'</u> ON THAR FER MOVIN' YER CREATION AROUND...

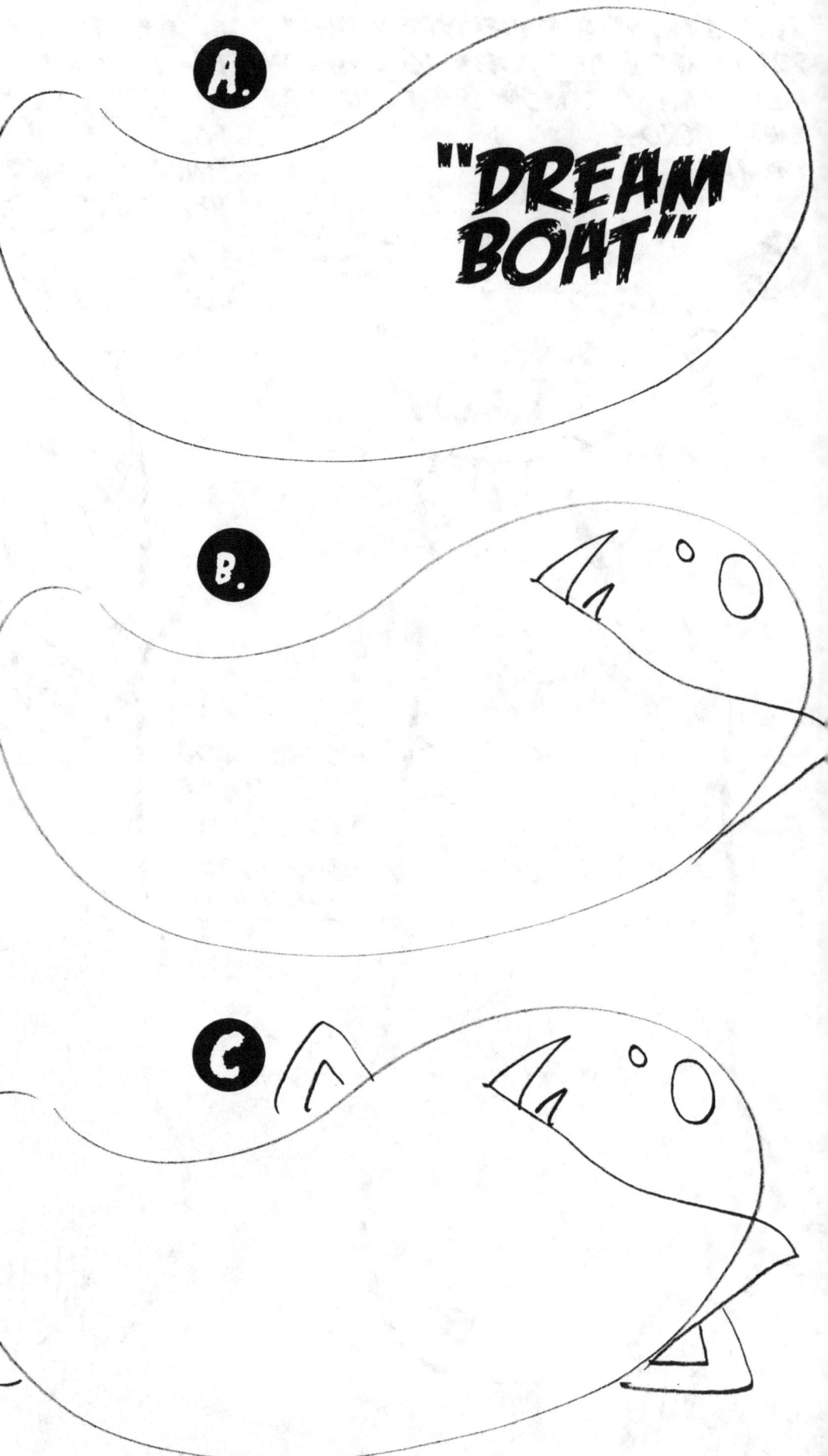

"DREAM BOAT"

MONSTERS, FER WHUT THEY ARE, LAHK TA LOOK GOOD TOO! THIS GUY IS OBVI-
OUSLY EXPECTIN' TA GET LUCKY WID TH' LADIES! TOO BAD HE'S PACKIN' A LOAD
IN THEM SHORTS, THO"!

D.

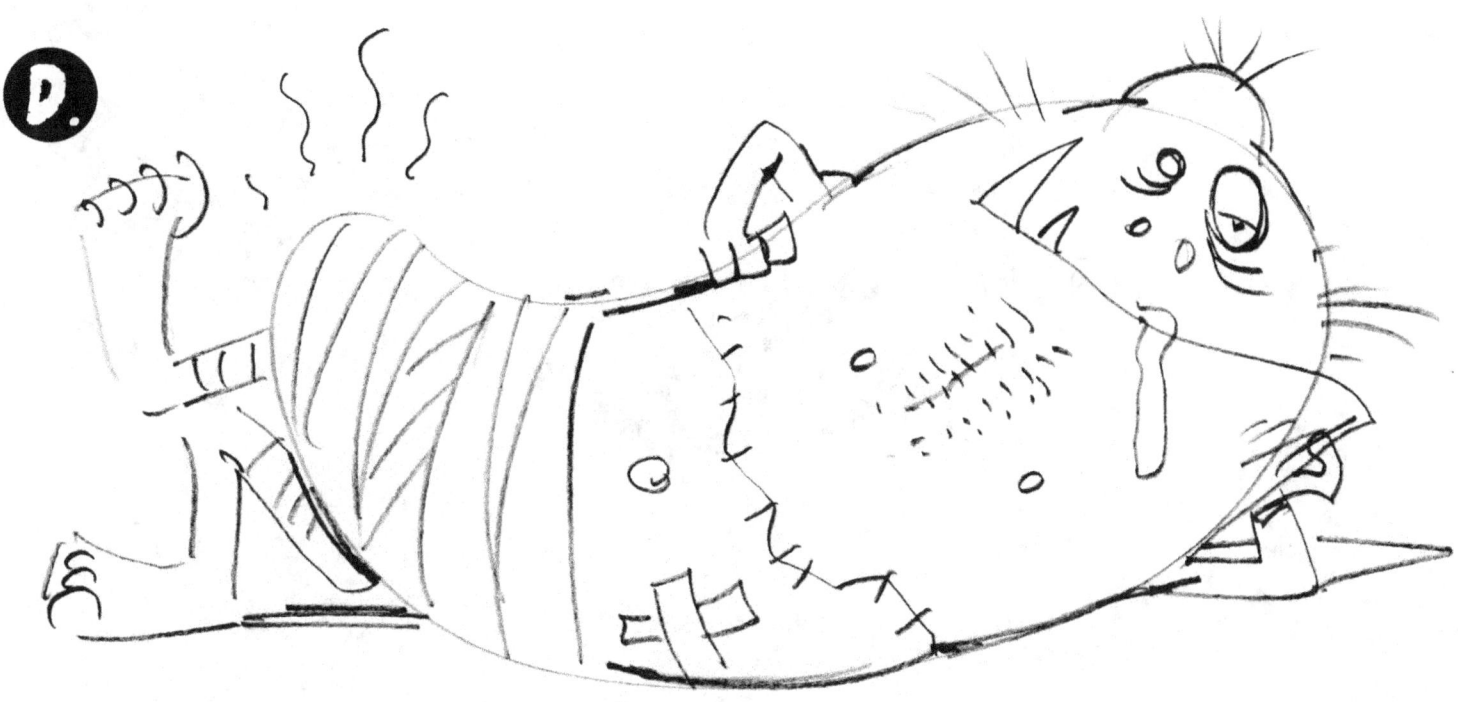

NOW YA KIN SEE HOW VON HOFFY ADDED STUFF IN <u>INK</u> THAT WARNT IN TH' <u>PEN-
CILS</u>! AN' BEE-HOLED THAT **BRAIN BUMP**, KIDS! THE OL' MAD SCIENTIST ALMOS'
FERGOT TA PLANT THAT SUCKER IN THAR! BWAH-HA!

E.

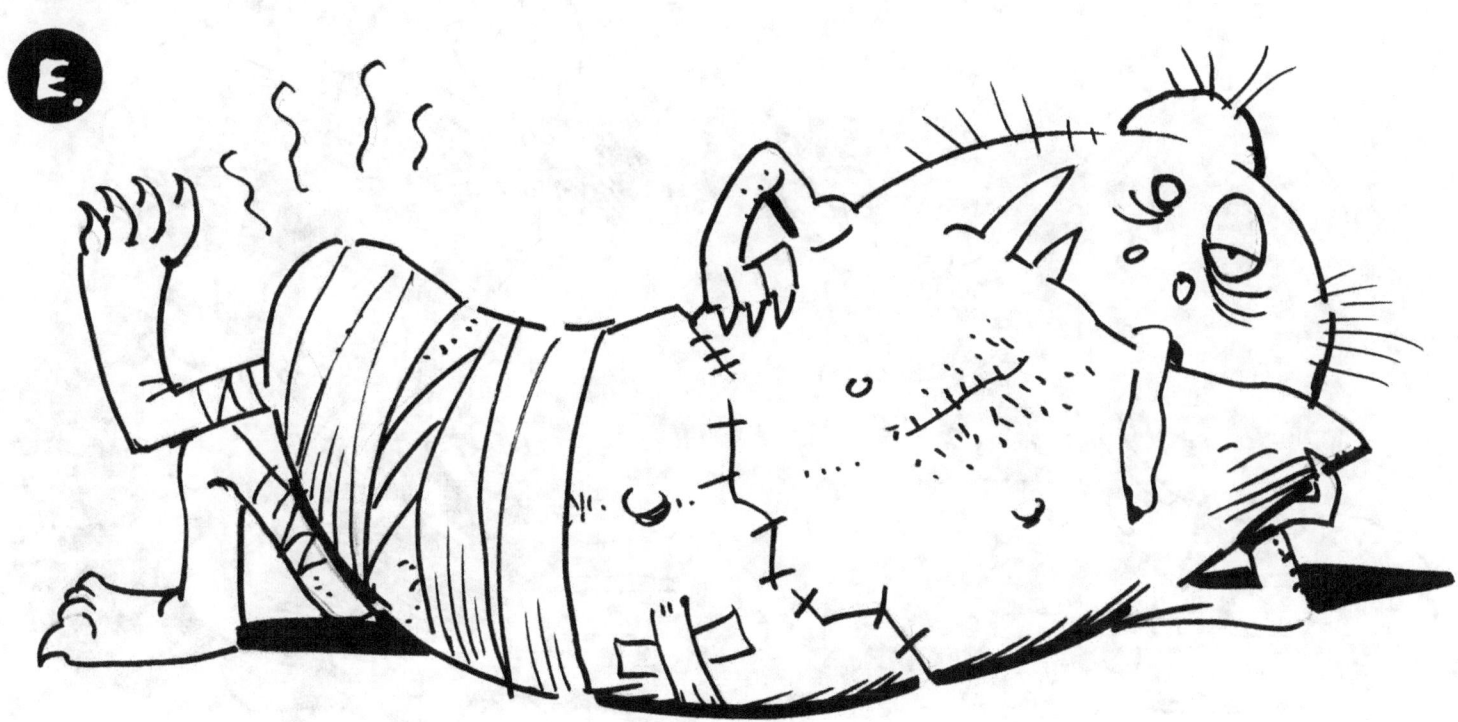

NOW YA MOVE UP TA DOIN' **TWO** STUPID SHAPES **TAGETHER**! HERE'S A **SAUSAGE** WID A **LIDDLER BLOB** ATTACHED...

YA DO TH' SAME SORTA **MOUTH** AN' EYES THANG, THEN ADD OTHER JUNK LIKE MEBBE SUM **WEIRD LOCOMOTION**!

"SPEED DEMON"

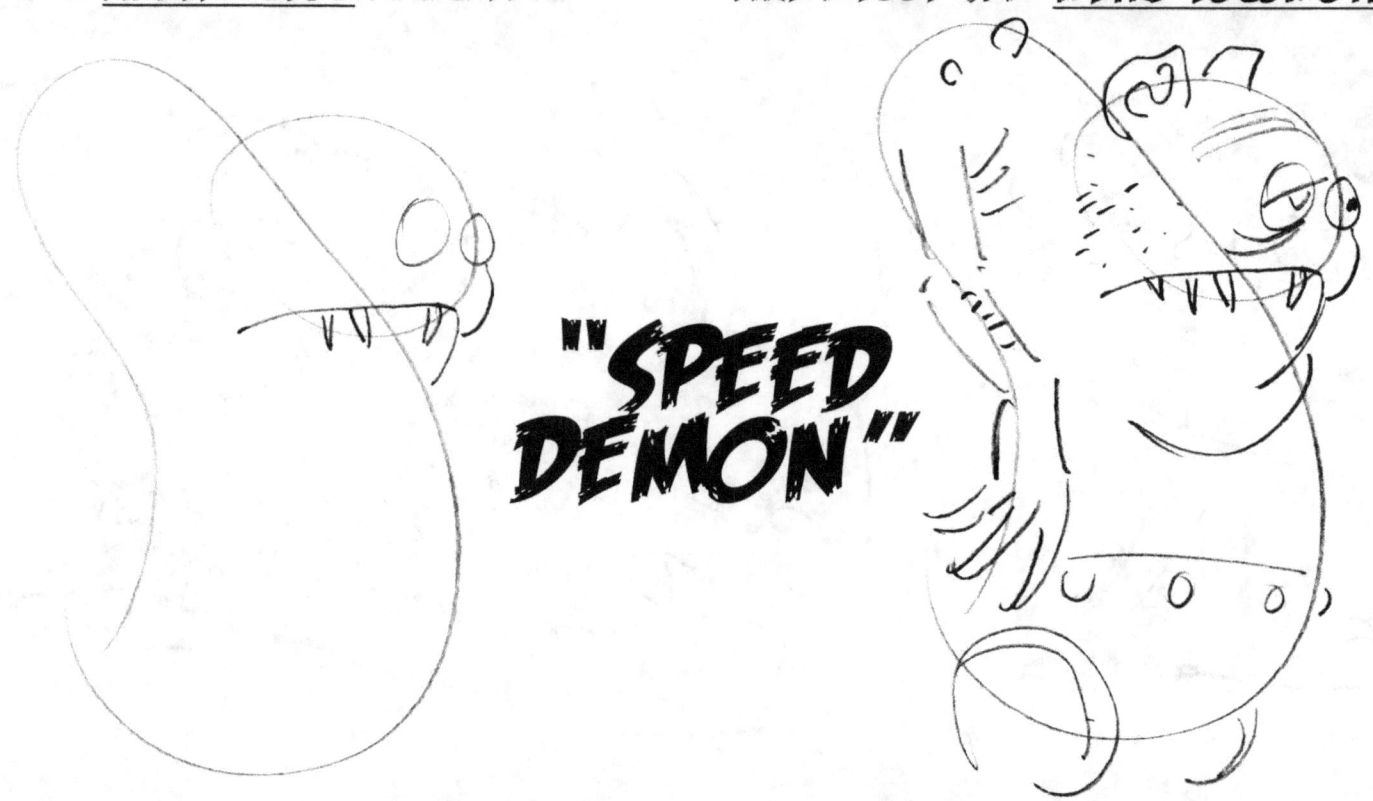

HERE WE GOTS THA FINAL LIDDLE DETAILS STUCK ON AND SOME **MOTION LINES** AN' PUFFS O' SMOKE! **ZOOM**!

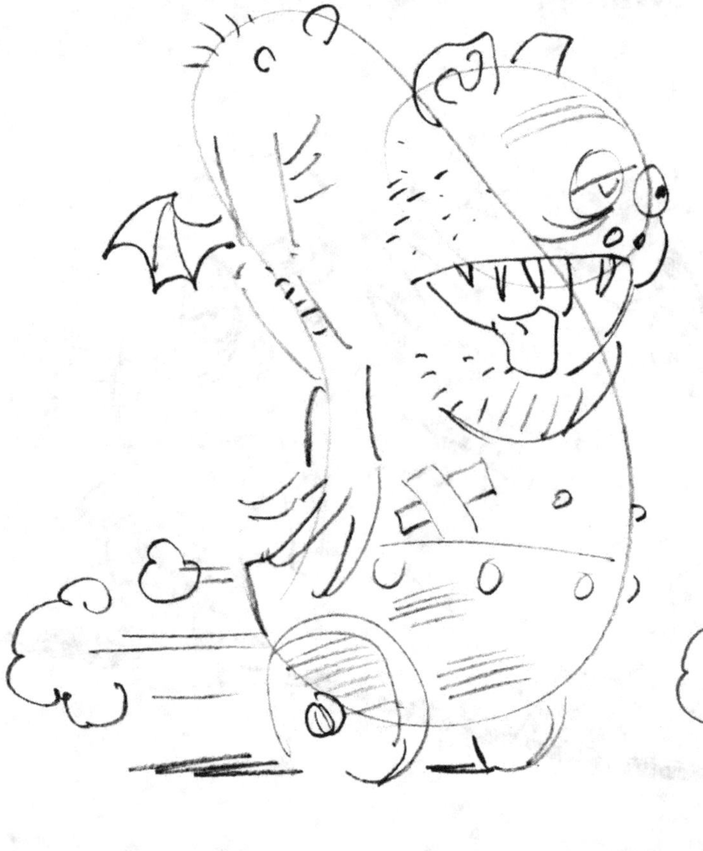

THEN **INK IT**! LOOKIT HOW TH' BIG, BLACK **SHADOW BLOB** MAKES THIS SPEED DEMON STICK OUT IN 3-D?

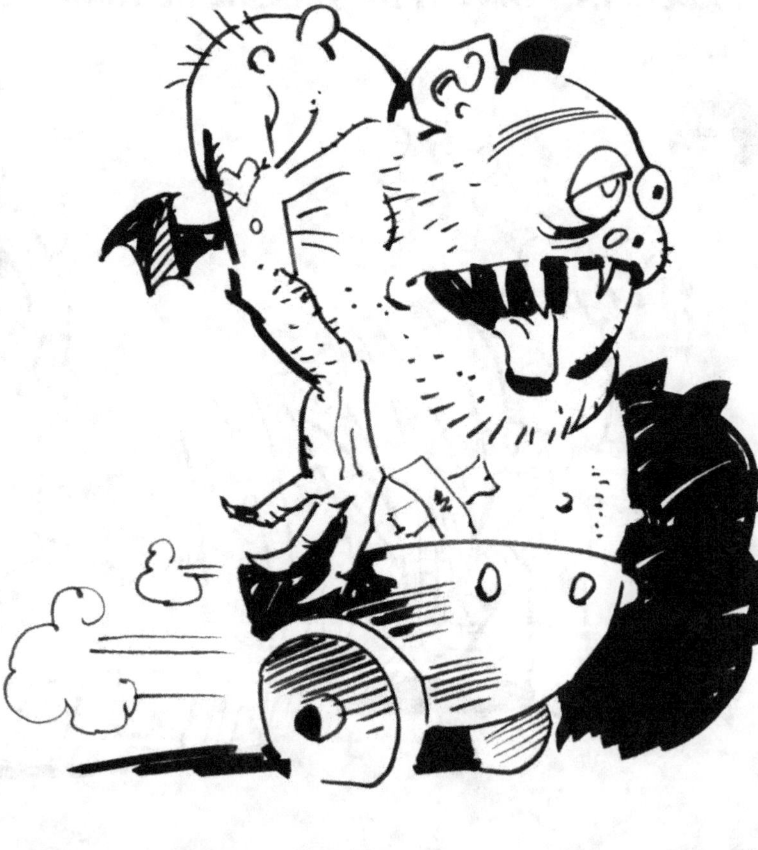

"BABY SITTER"

ARE YA READY TA MOVE UP TA **THREE BLOBS** NOW? CAN YA **HANDLE IT?**

YA DON'T HAFTA PUT 'EM WHERE **WE** DID, **ENNYWHERES** IS FINE!

JUST REMEMBER TA **THINK STUPID!**

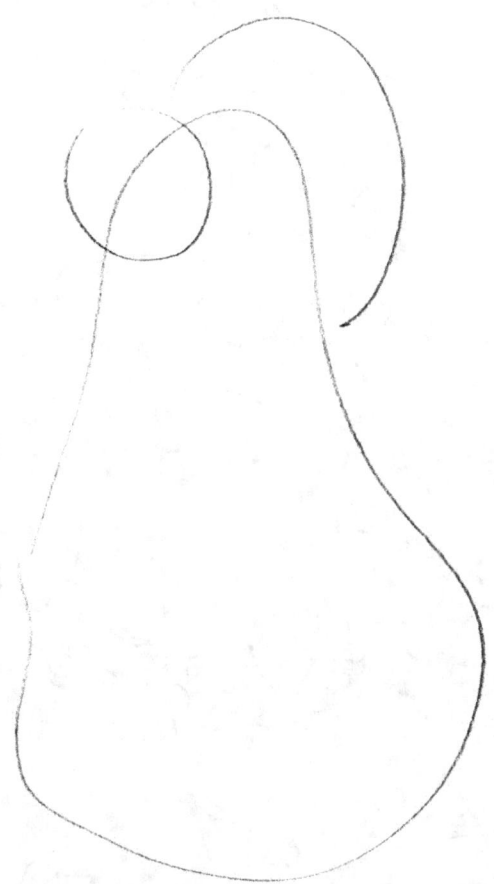

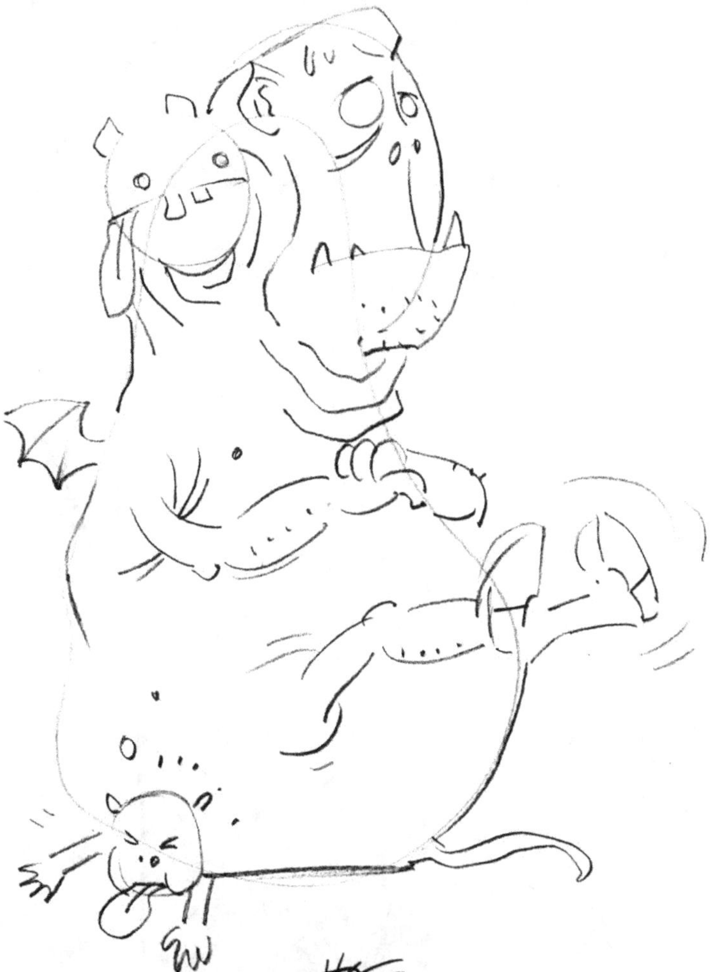

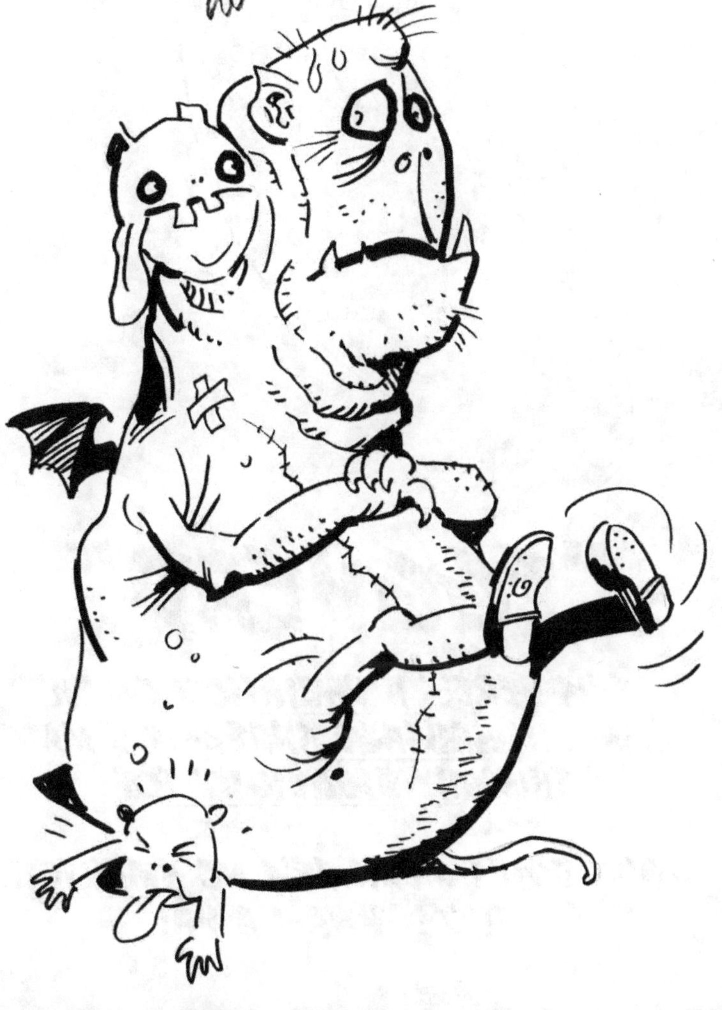

AN' BY ALL MEANS, COVER EVER SKWARE INCH O' YER MONSTER WID **WEIRD STUFF!**

MAKE THEM **STITCHES** LOOK LIKE A **ROAD MAP** O' TRAIN TRACKS!

BWA-HA-HAAAAA!

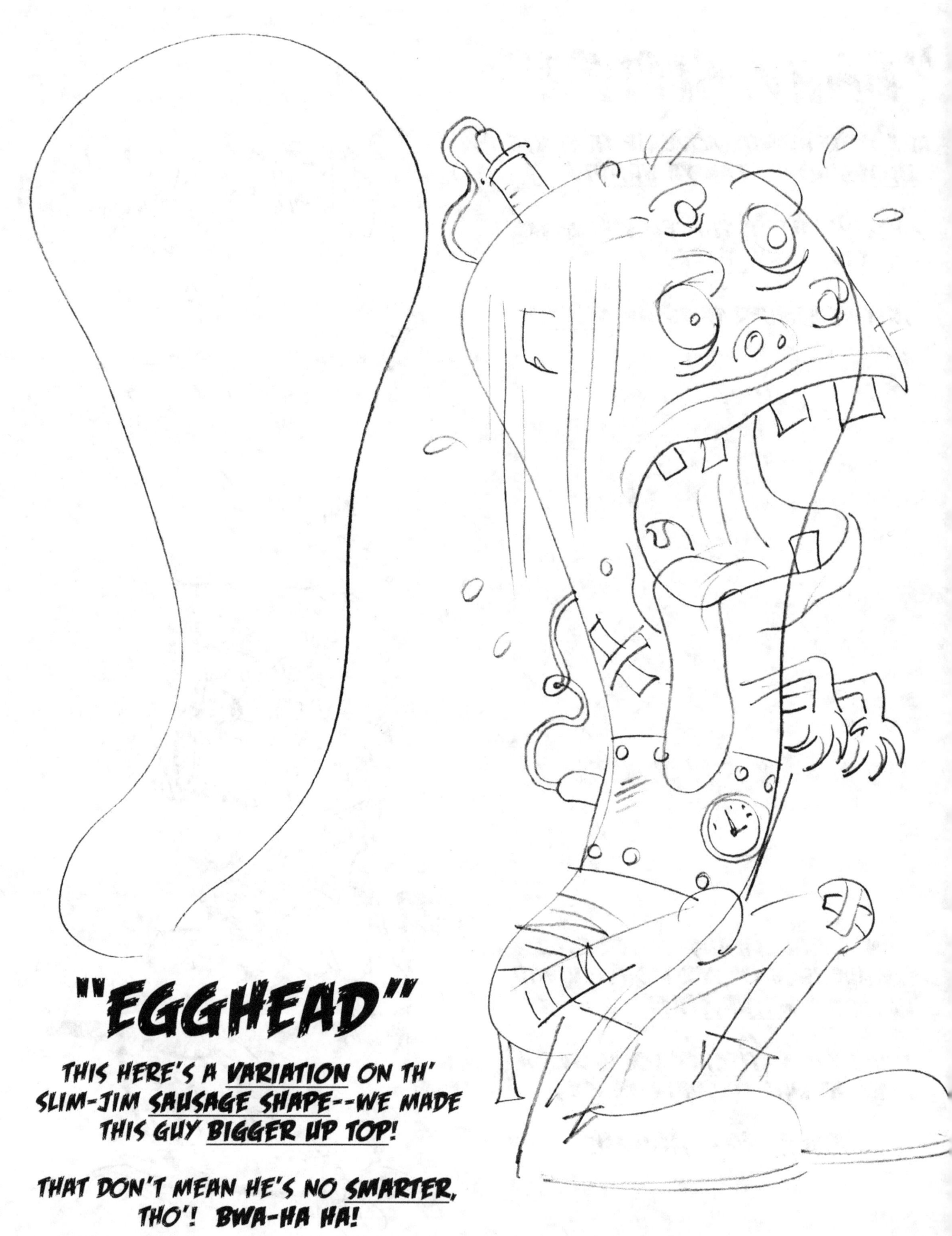

"EGGHEAD"

THIS HERE'S A VARIATION ON TH'
SLIM-JIM SAUSAGE SHAPE--WE MADE
THIS GUY BIGGER UP TOP!

THAT DON'T MEAN HE'S NO SMARTER,
THO'! BWA-HA HA!

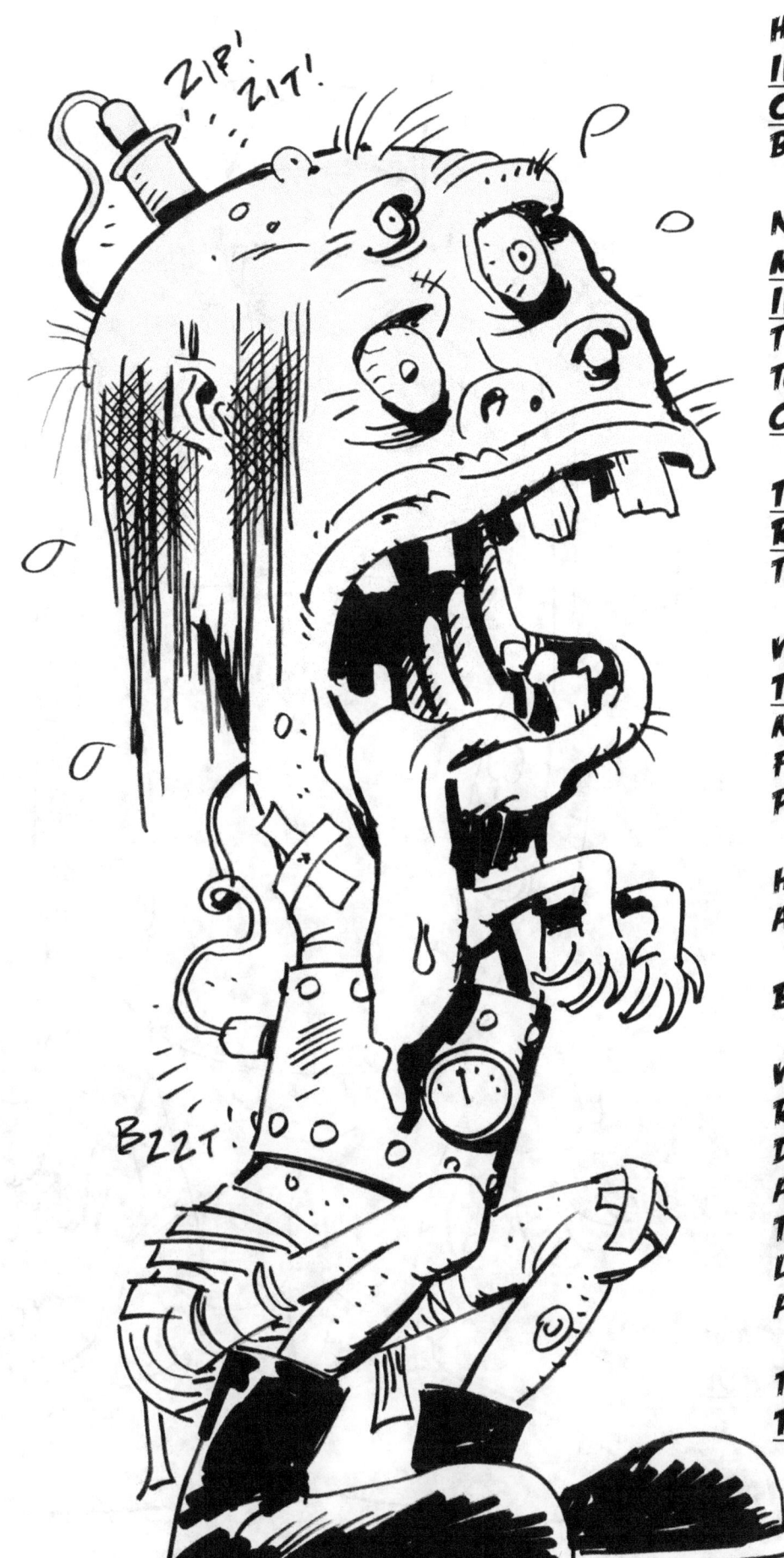

HERE'S DARLIN' BOY ALL INKED UP AN' READY FER CHURCH ON SUNDAY! BWA-HA-HAAA!

NOTICE HE WE MADE TH' MOUTH LINE AKSHULLY CUT INTA TH' SAUSAGE THIS TIME? YOU CAN DO DIS TOO, AND MAKE' SUM BIG OL' GAPIN' HOLES!

TEETH SHOULD BE NICE AN' ROTTEN, OR OPTIONAL ALL-TAGETHER!

WE ALSO USED SOME ELEC-TRONIC GEAR ON THIS MONSTER, YA KNOW VICTOR FRANKENSTEIN WOULD AP-PROVE O' DAT!

HEY, AN' SOUNDY FECKS ARE OKAT, TOO! FZIT!!!

BWA-HA-HAA!

WE SHOULD SAY FER TH' RECORD THAT ALLA THESE DRAWIN'S IN THIS BOOK ARE TH' SAME SIZE AS TH' PRICELESS ORIGINALS LOCKED AWAY IN THE VAULTS AT H.I.!

THAT'S HOFFMAN INTERNA-TIONAL! BWA-HA-HAAAAA!

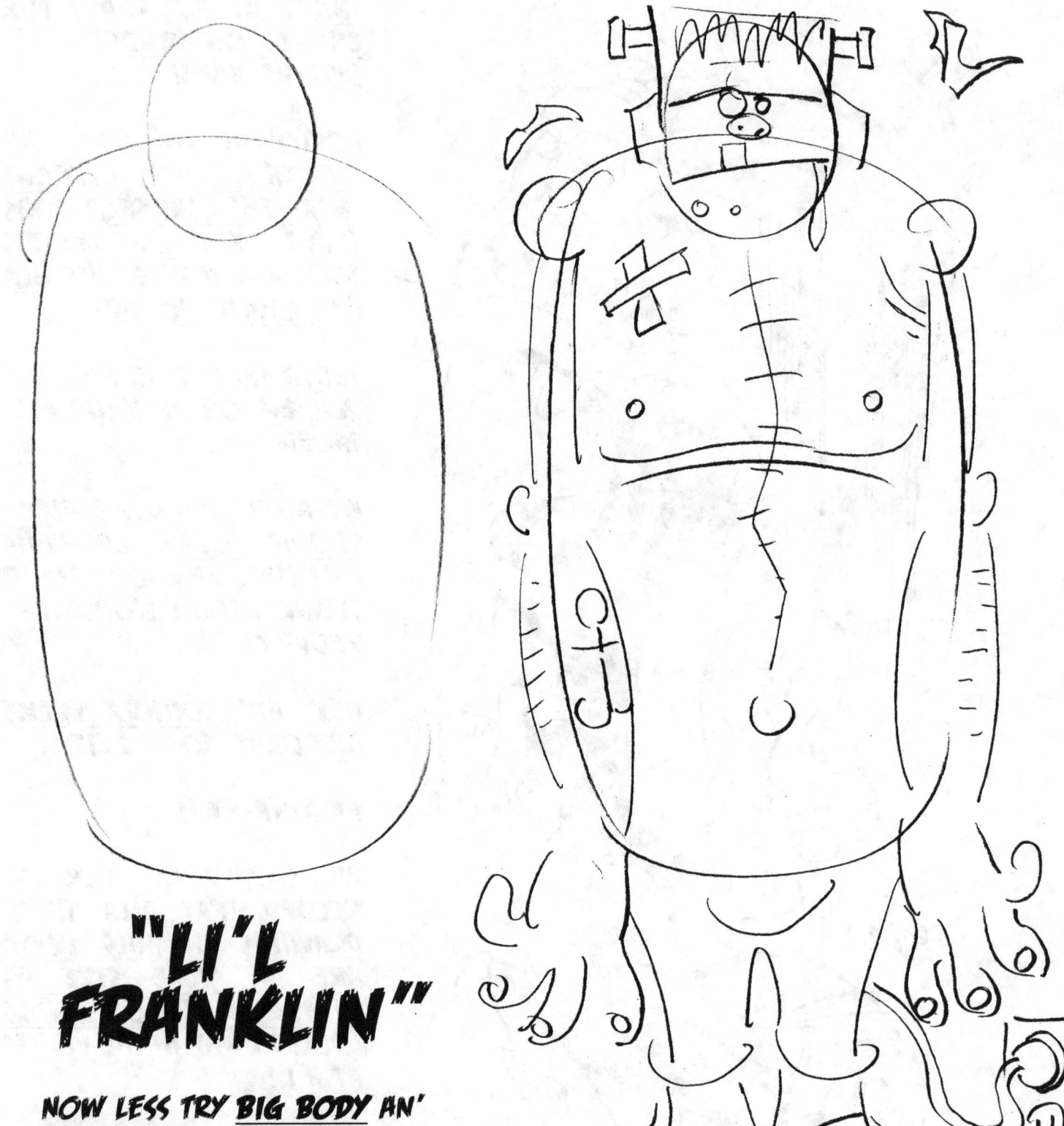

"LI'L FRANKLIN"

NOW LESS TRY **BIG BODY** AN' **TEENY HAID!** MAKE THET **BOD** LIKE A **TATER SACK!**

LOOKIT TH' **ARMS**, WE USED TH'OL' **TUBE METHOD** BUT ADDED **BULBY BALLS** AT TH' **SOCKETS!**

WHEN YA DO YER **BLACKS**, MAKE SURE YER PIC "READS" FRUM ACROSS TH' ROOM! OR JUS' SQUINT AT IT! CAN YA STILL TELL WHUT IT **IS**? BWAH-HA-HA!

WE ADDED LOTSA STUFF YA WERE'T SPECKTIN'! BWA-HA-HA! MAKE AS MANY LINES AS YA NEED, **HAIR** AN' STUBBLE WILL MAKE YER MONSTER A REAL **SLOB**!

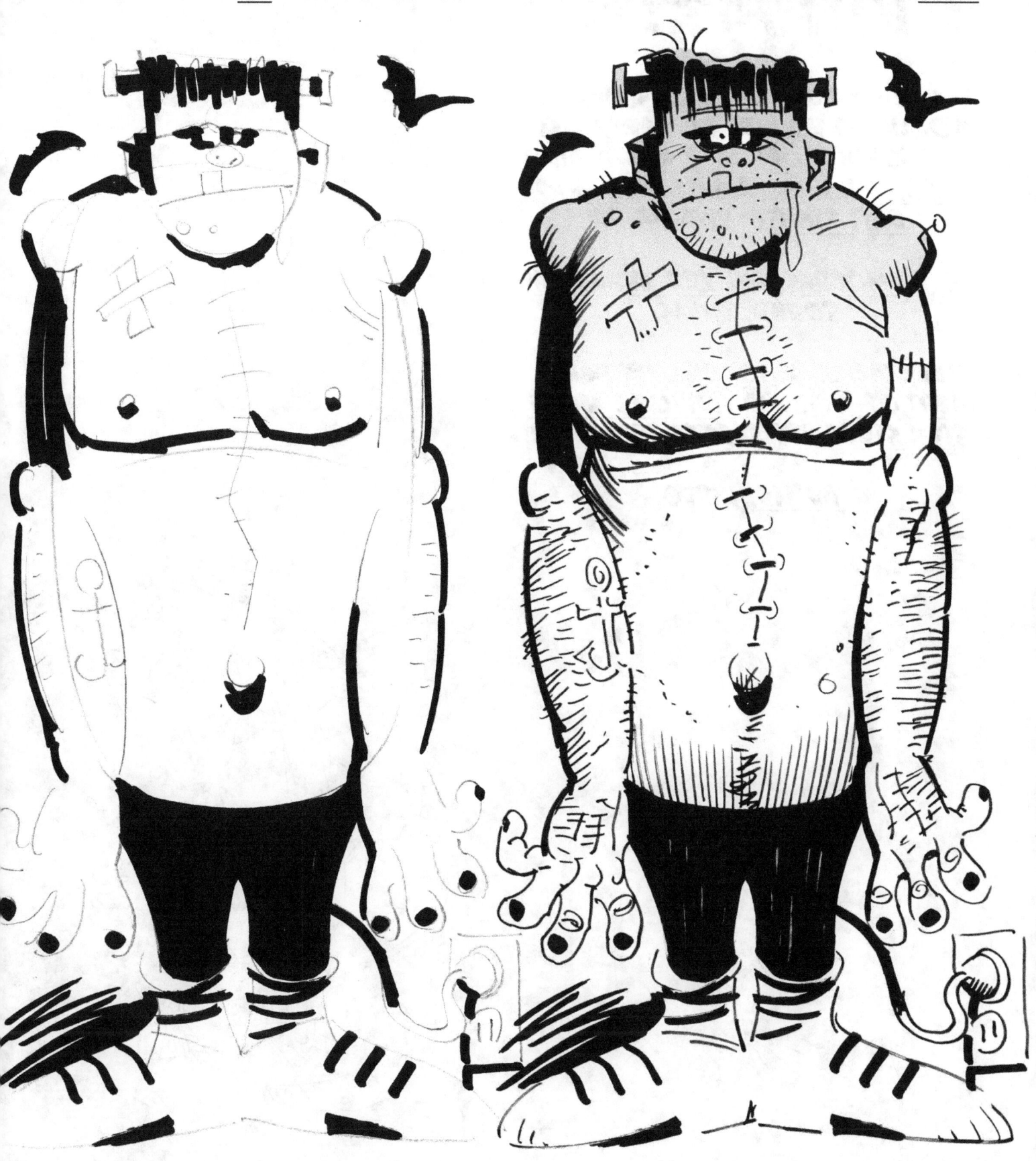

"HEY, YA BIG APE!"

IT'S QUITE TROO DAT BLOBS MAKE DA WORLD GO ROUND, TH' EARTH ITSEF IS A SORTA BLOB! YA KNOW IT AIN'T REALLY ROUND, RIGHT? YOU NOO DAT, RIGHT? BWA-HA-HA!

SO'S AMOEBAS, AN' YER GRANDMA! ROUND, DAT IS!

HERE WE GO WIT BLOBS YET AGAIN, TWO OF 'EM, WID TIDPICKLE MONSTER STUFF ADDED ONTA DEM LATER!

AD LIB, KIDDO!

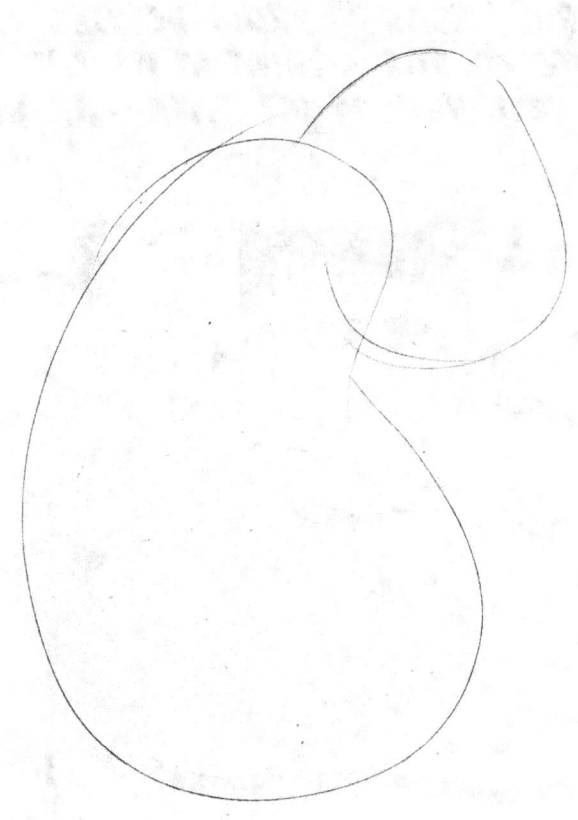

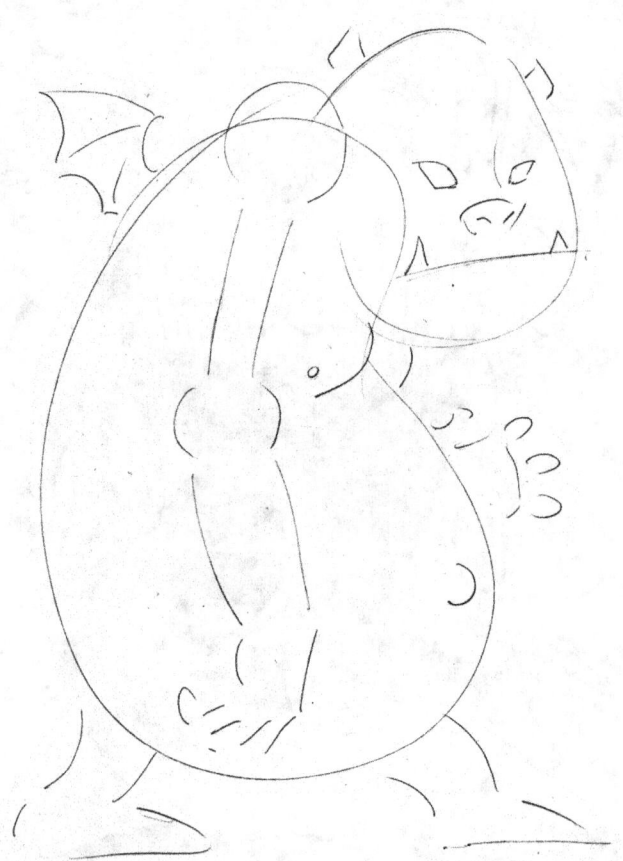

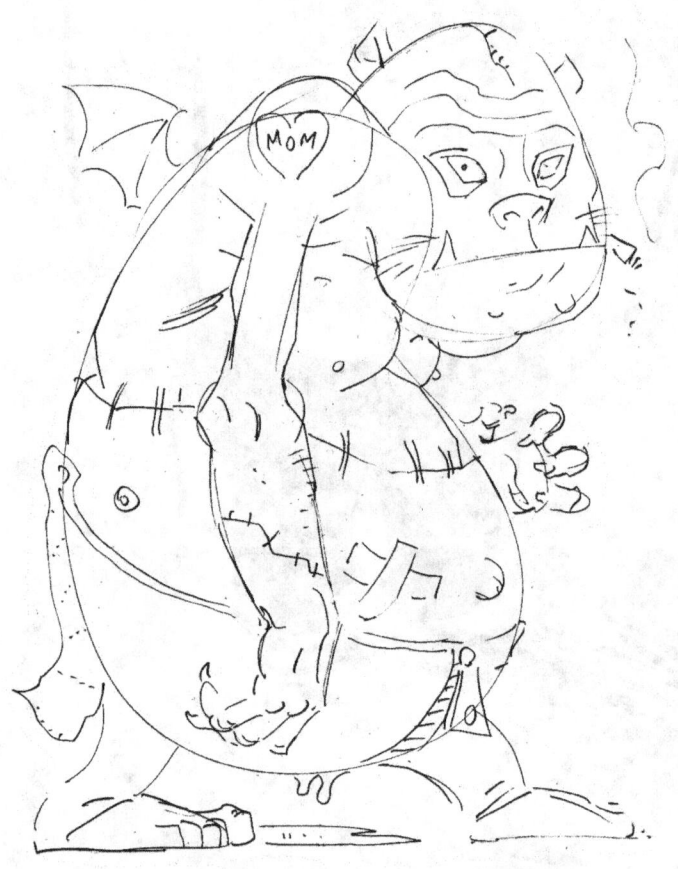

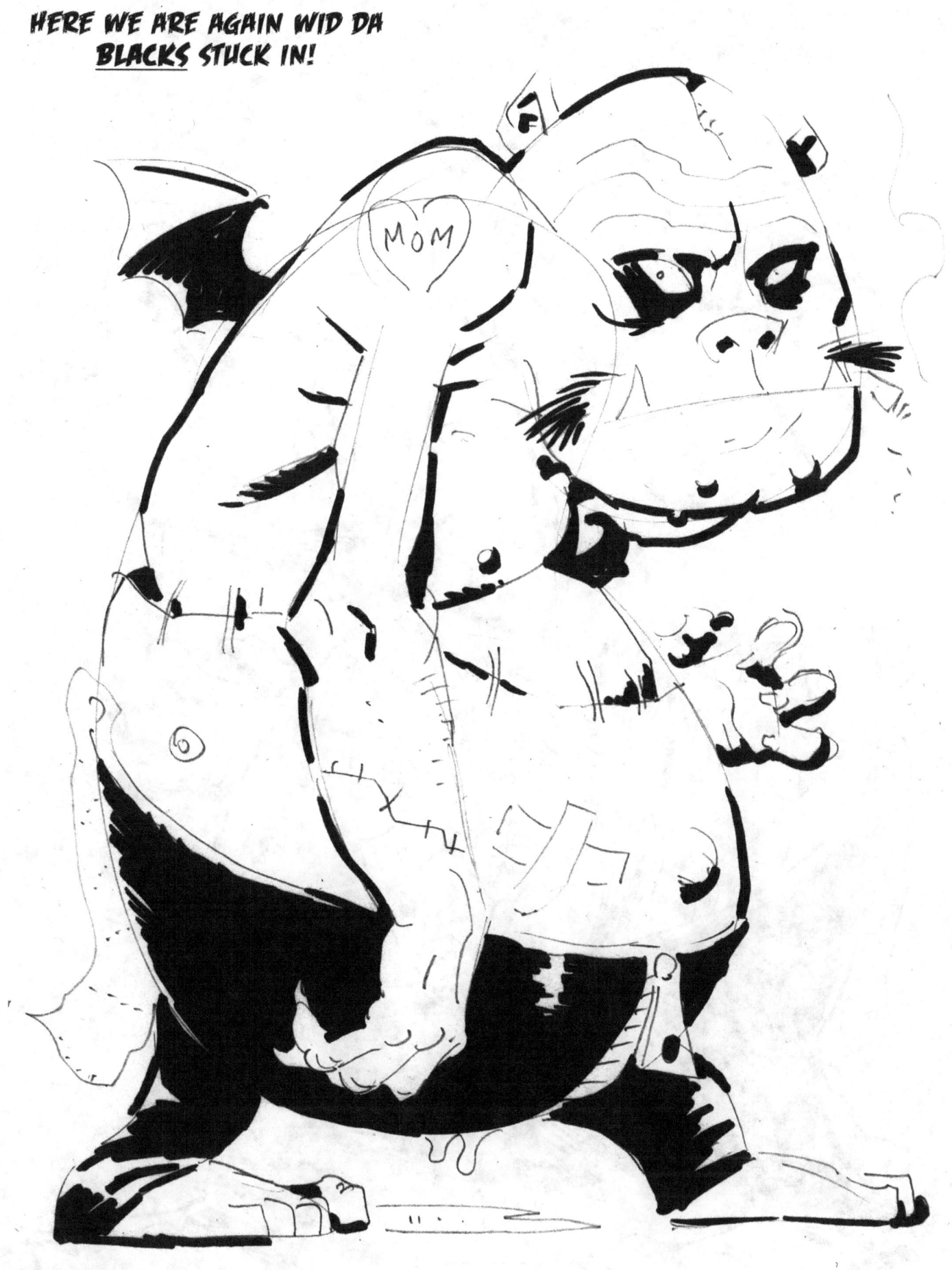

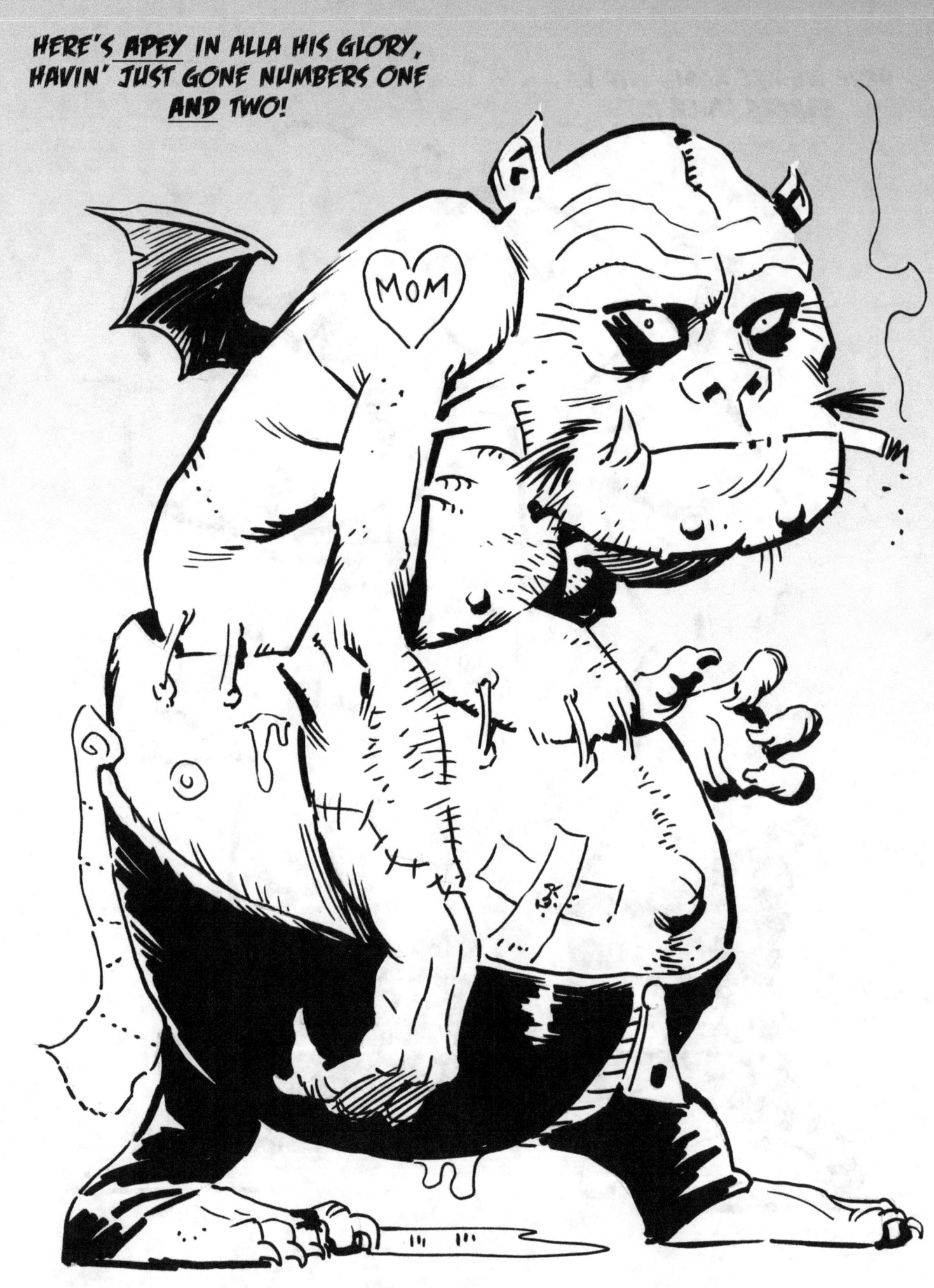

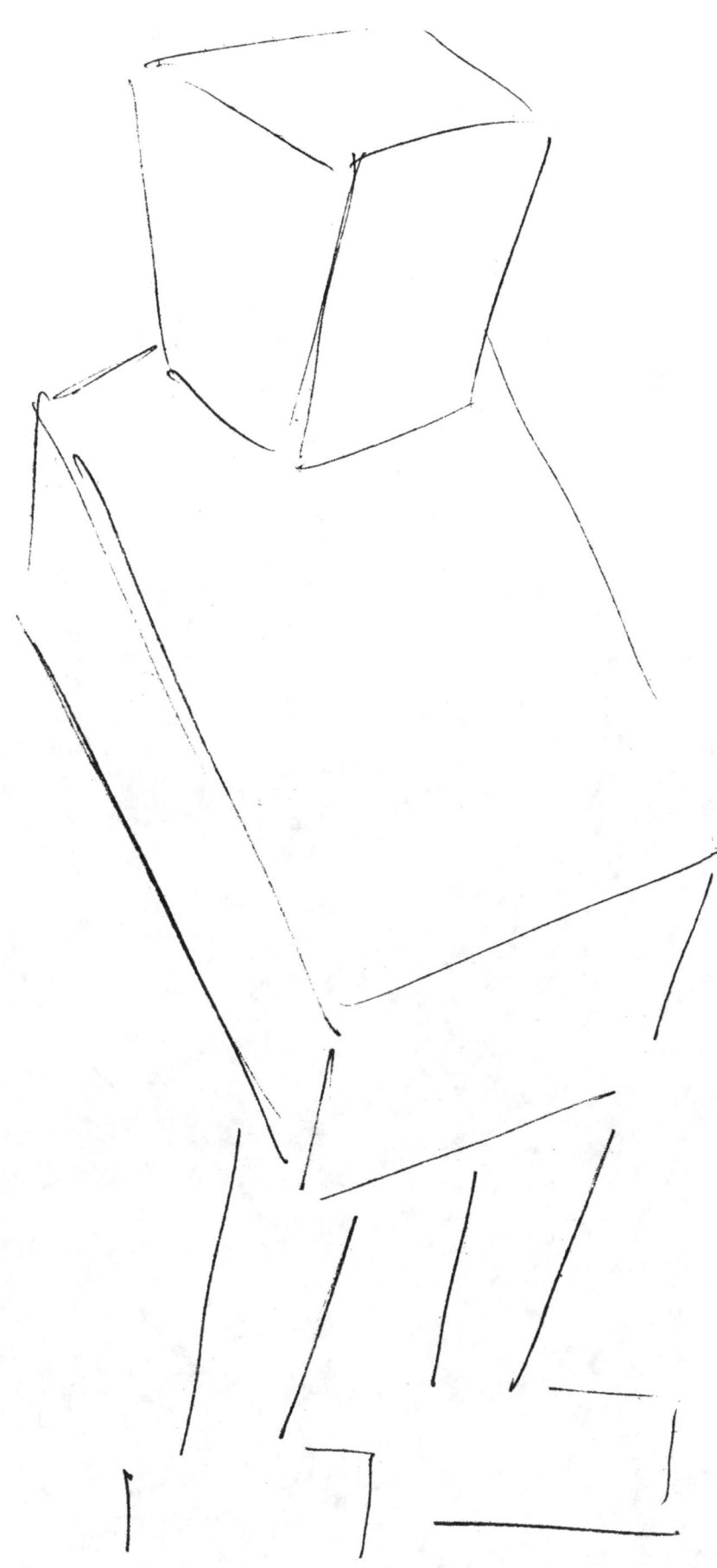

"BLOBBY BOBBY"

NOW, _YOU_ MAY NOT THINK _BLOBS_ ARE ALL THAT _FUNNY!_

WELP, WHY NOT TRY SOME OTHER SHAPES--MORE SQUARERER ONES?

BWA-HA-HA!

NOW LOOKAT DIS GUY ON YER LEFT-- WE USED A BIG OL' _BOX_ FER HIS _SEXY BOD_...

AN' ONE FER HIS BIG _OL'_ HEAD, TOO!

SURE, MAKE _EVERTHIN'_ SQUARE, YA MAD MONSTER-MAKER!

COZ WE'Z GONNA _BLOB DIS GUY UP_ ON TH' NEXT FEW PAGES!

BWA-HA-HAAAAA!

>CHOKE!<

SEE? DIS AIN'T SO HARD!

JUS' BLOB BOB-O UP LIKE HE'S BEEN EATIN' NUTTIN' BUT DOUGHNUTS FER A FEW YEARS! BELCHH!

MAKE HIM PUFFY, PUDGY AND DISGUSTIN' LOOKIN'!

VISIT ANY GROCERY STORE IN NORTH AMERICA FER PLENTIFUAL LIVE MODELS!

BWA-HA-HA!

SEE HOW DEM BOX SHAPES UNDERNEATH HELP GIVE ROBERT SOME SUPPORT UNDER HIS BLOBBY 'N' QUAKEY FRAME?

BWA-HA-HA!

I'LL SAY IT AGIN!

BWA-HA-HA!

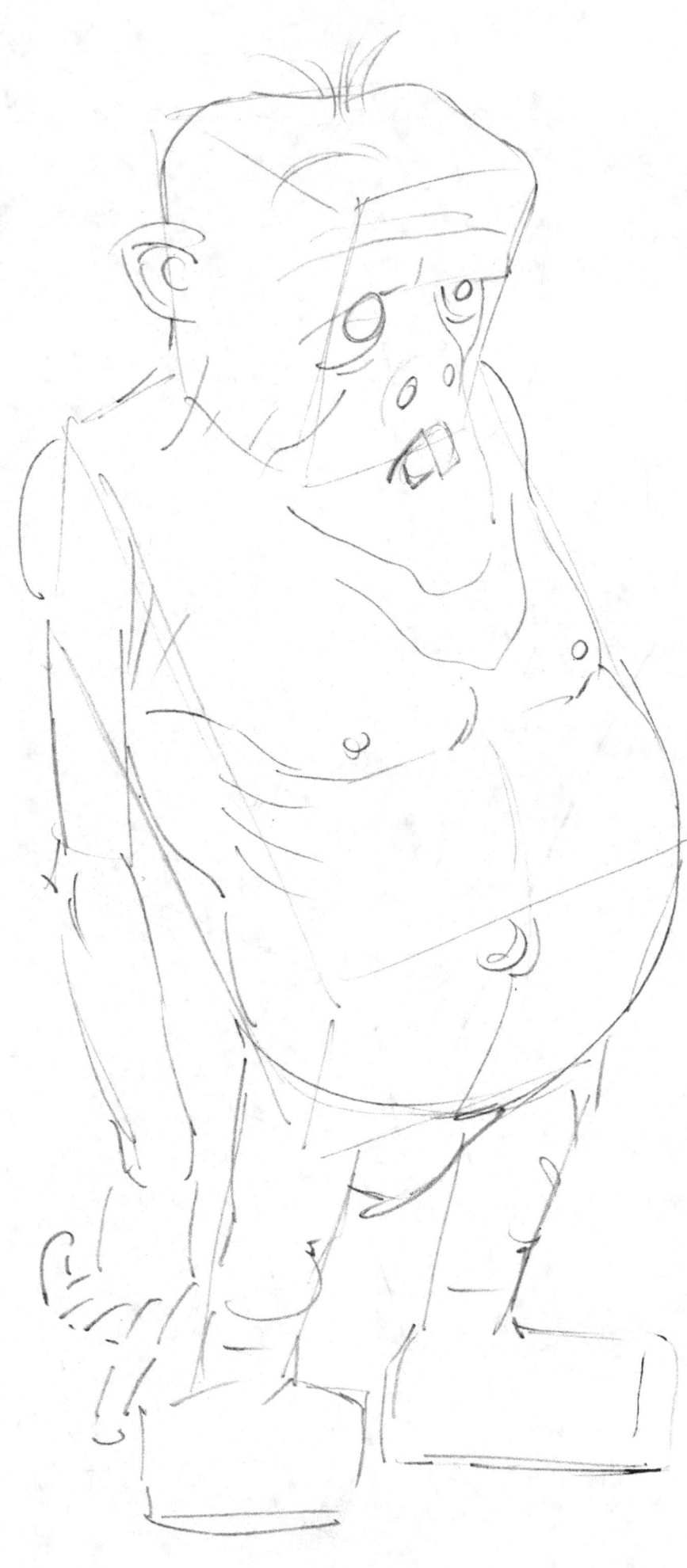

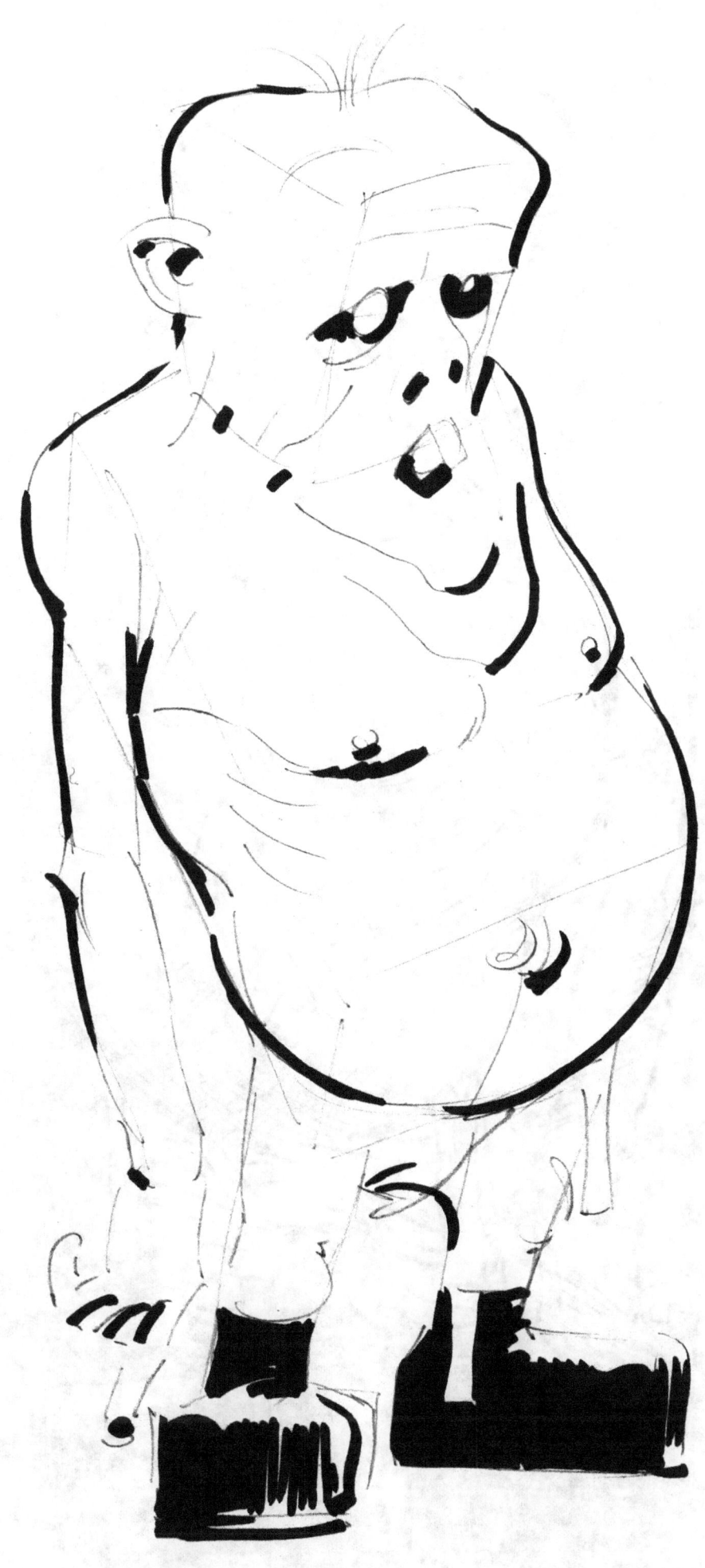

NOW WE'RE INTA TH' **BLACK SHAPES** LIKE ON ALLA TH' **OTHER** DRAWINGS YA DONE DID SO FAR!

MAKE IT "**READ**" FRUM ACROSS TH' **TOMB**, GOON!

SURE, THEM **CHEAP SHARPIE MARKERS** END LINES KINDA **CHUNKY**, BUT YOU KIN SHARPEN THET UP WIT YER **FINE-POINT PAPERMATE**!

DON'T GIVE UP, OR WE WILL ALL **HATE YOU!**

YOU'LL BE **CURSED!**

AN' YOU'LL **HATE YERSELF!**

BWA-HA-HA!

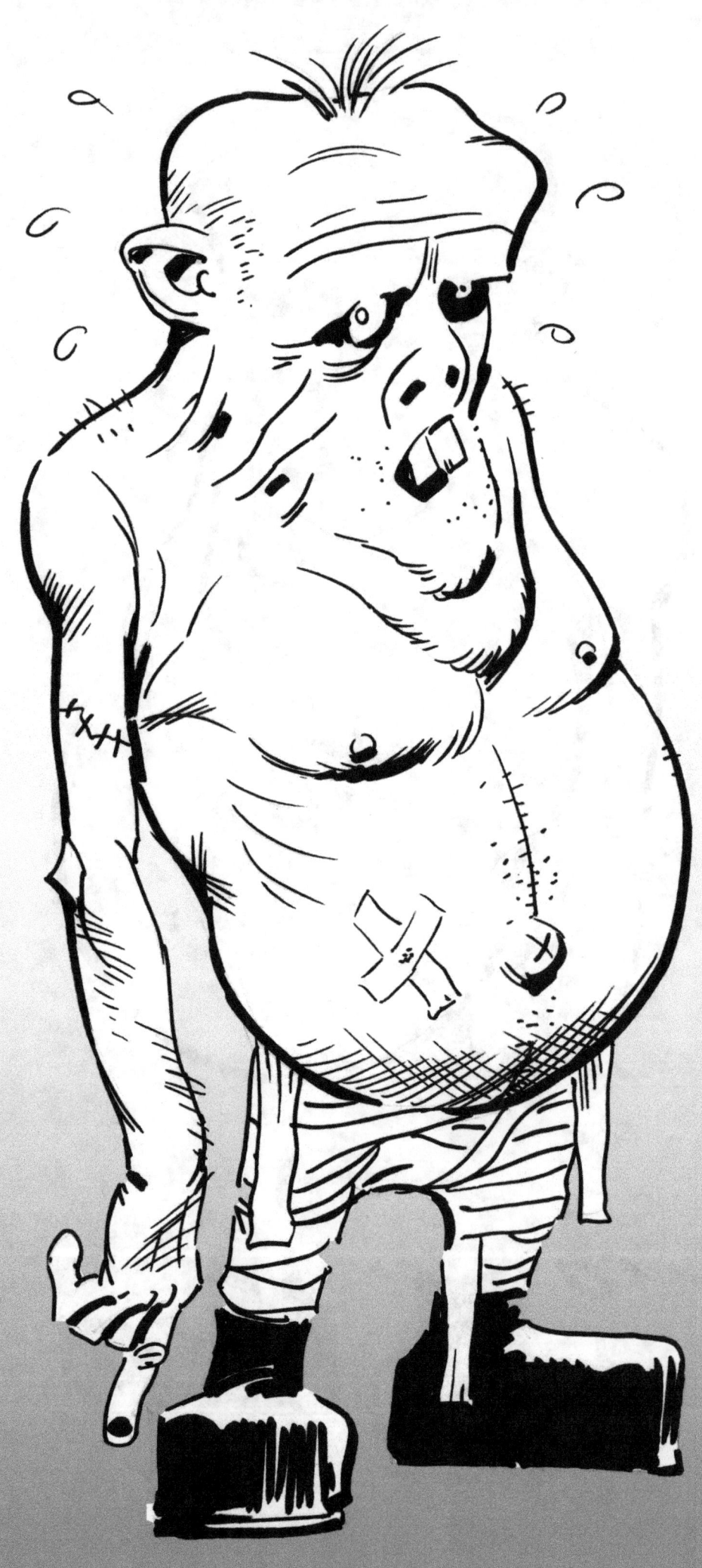

"LUMPY LOU"

MOST GUYS IN'
DIS HERE BOOK
ARE LUMPY-
LOOKIN',
BUT NUN MORE
SO DAN
LUMPY LOU
HERE!

HE'S TH'
KING LUMPSTER,
AND WE GONNA
LEARN TA
DRAW HIM!

REDDY?

EN GUARDE
WID DA
DUMB SHAPES,
DEN!

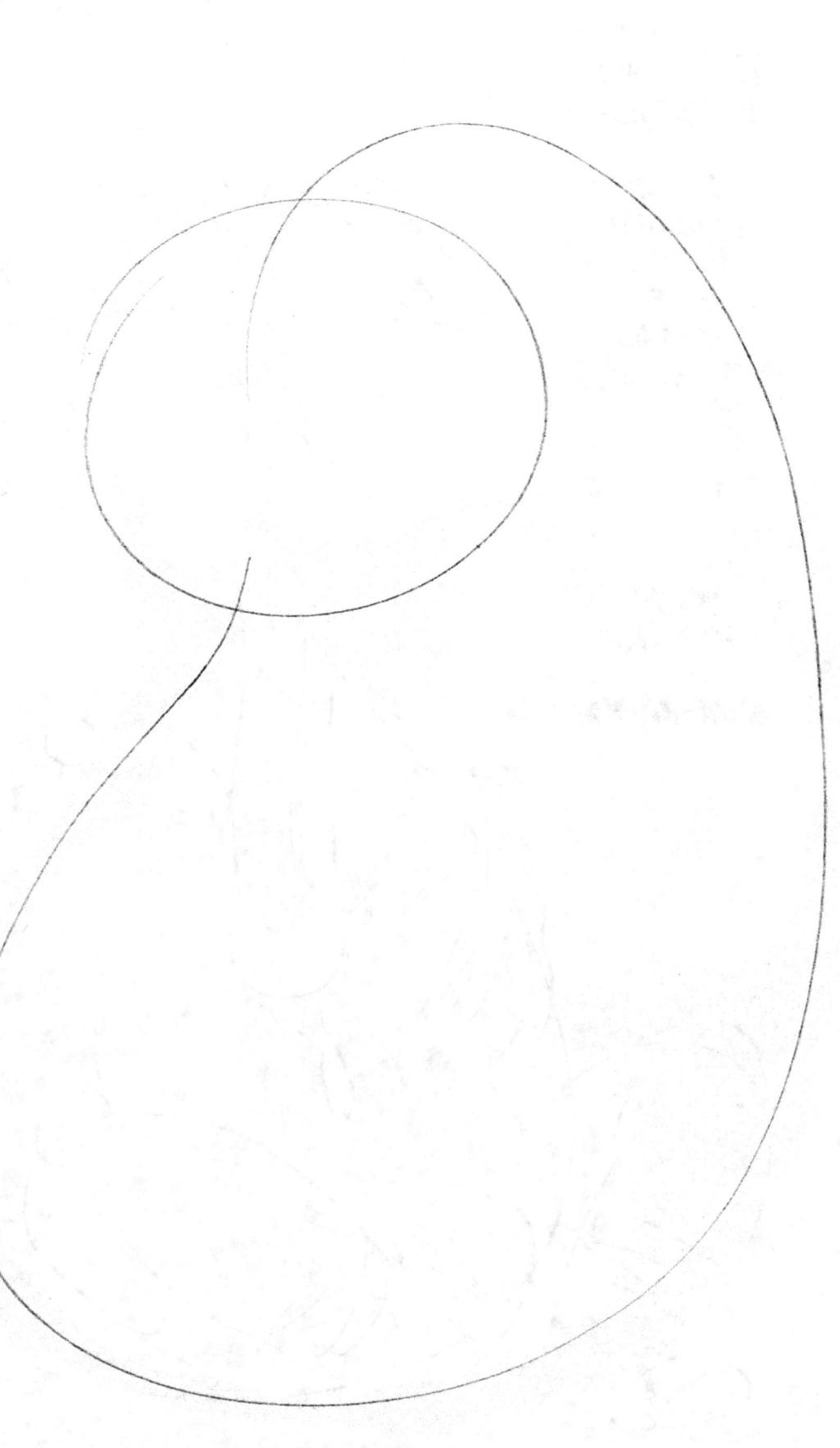

STEP TWO IS
WE DRAW IN
TH' DETAILS--

GOOSHY
EYEBALLS,
TONGUE
STUFF,
FUMBLY
FANGERS,
ET CETERA!

DON' FERGET
TH' WARTS!

WE ALL
GOTS 'EM!

BWA-HA-HA!

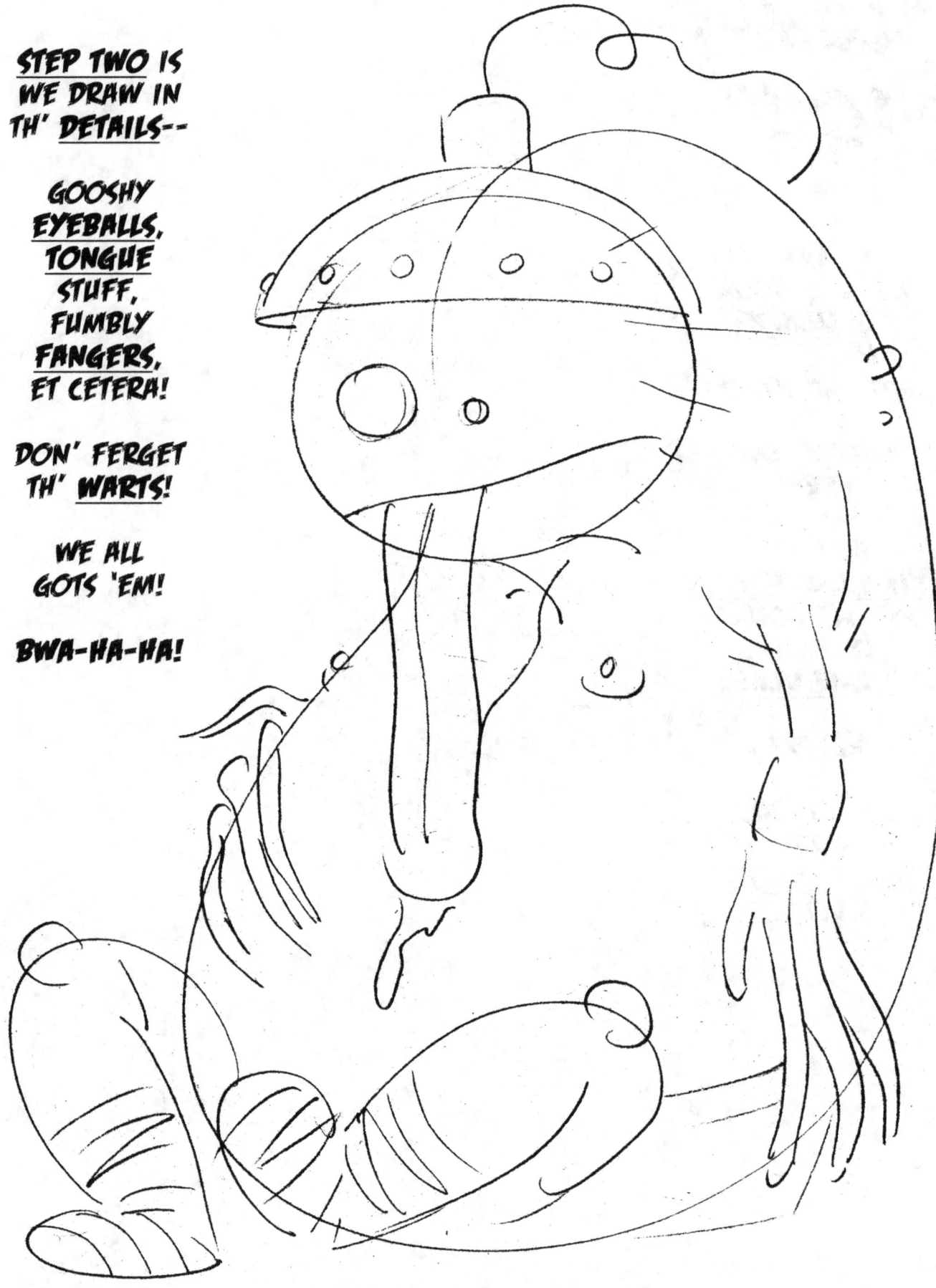

YER ALMOS' <u>DERE</u>, MONSTER MAKER!

JUS' SLAP IN DEM <u>GOOPY BLACK BITS</u> LIKE DOC VON HOFFY TOL' YA!

SEE HOW DAT <u>BIG, BLACK SHADDER</u> MAKES LUMPY'S <u>TONGUE POP OUT ATCHA?</u>

BWA-HA!

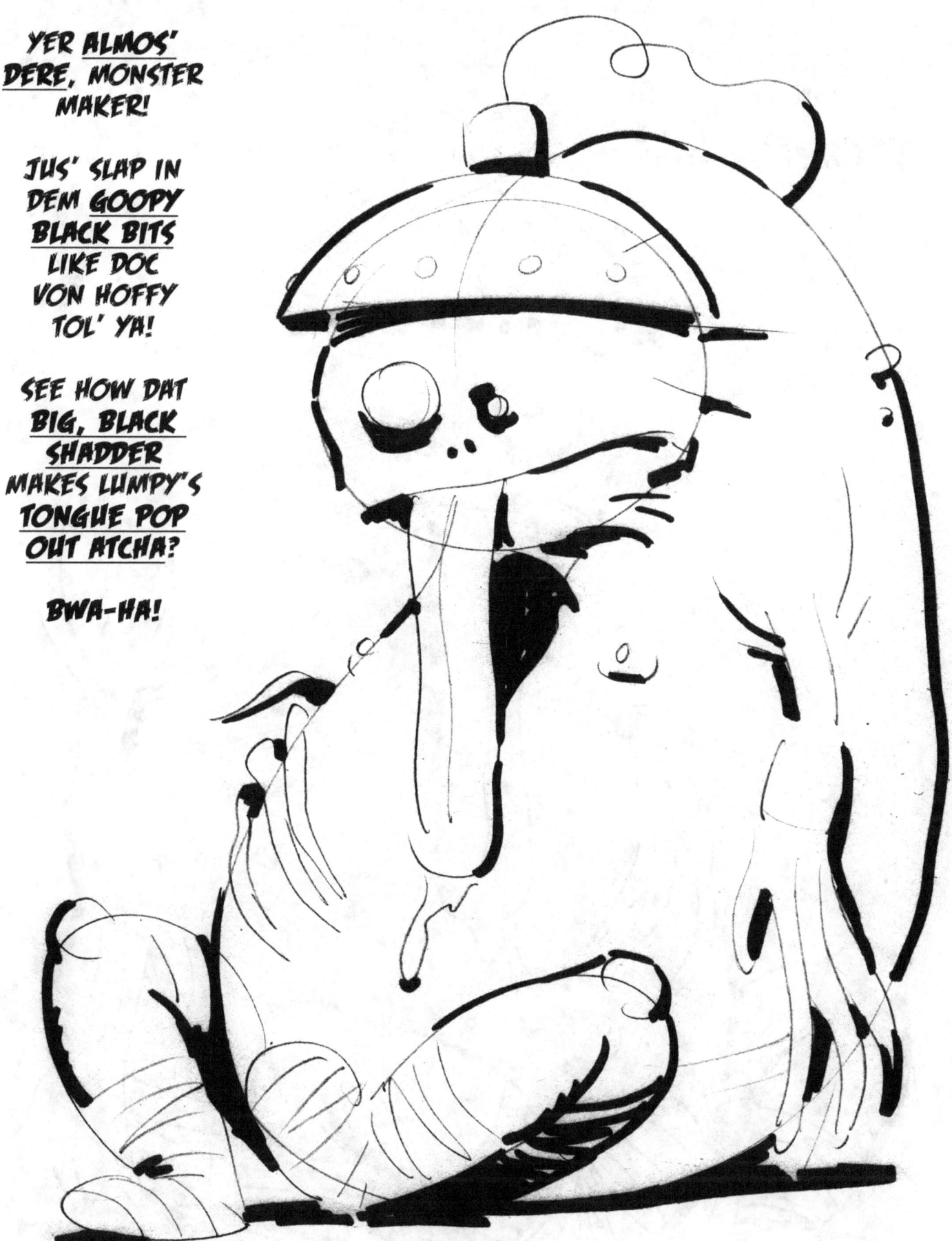

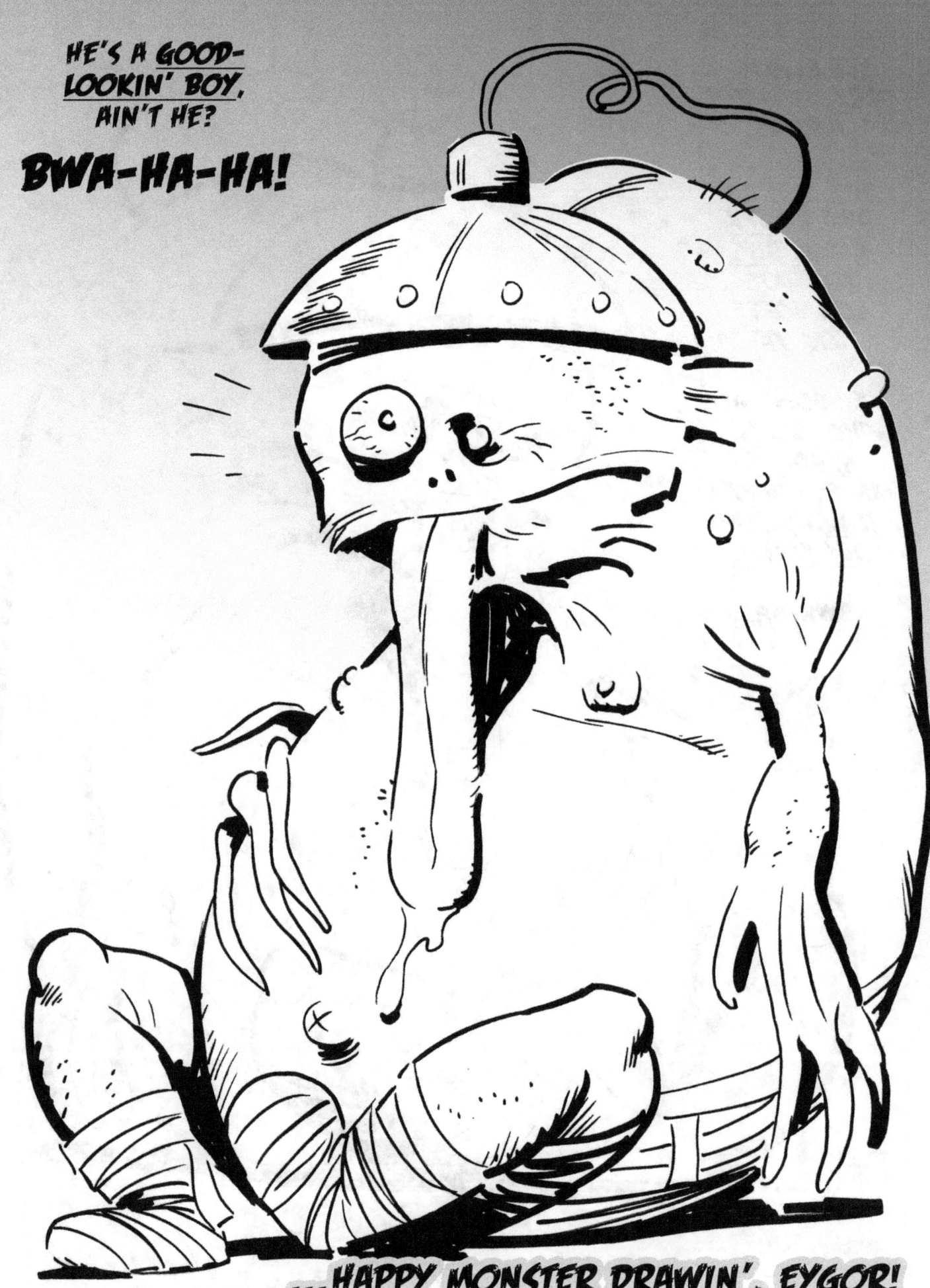